START-UP
DESIGN AND TECHNOLOGY

MAKING PUPPETS

Claire Llewellyn

Evans

Published by Evans Brothers Limited
2A Portman Mansions
Chiltern Street
London W1U 6NR

© Evans Brothers Limited 2006

Produced for Evans Brothers Limited by
White-Thomson Publishing Ltd.,
Bridgewater Business Centre, 210 High Street,
Lewes, East Sussex BN7 2NH

Printed in China by WKT Company Limited

Editor: Dereen Taylor
Consultants: Nina Siddall, Head of Primary School
Improvement, East Sussex; Norah Granger, former
primary head teacher and senior lecturer in Education,
University of Brighton
Designer: Leishman Design

British Library Cataloguing in Publication Data
Llewellyn, Claire
    Puppets. - (Start-up design & technology)
    1.Puppets - Juvenile literature 2.Puppet making
    Juvenile literature
    I.Title II.Spilsbury, Louise
    745.5'9224

ISBN-10: 0 237 53027 9
13-digit ISBN (from 1 Jan 2007) 978 0 237 53027 3

Acknowledgements:
Special thanks to the following for their help and
involvement in the preparation of this book: Staff and
pupils at Coldean Primary School, Brighton and
Hassocks Infants School, Hassocks.

Picture Acknowledgements:
Chris Fairclough Worldwide 15 (left); Corbis 5 (bottom),
14, 15 (right).
All other photographs by Chris Fairclough.

Special thanks to:
Hodder Children's Books for the use of *The Gingerbread
Man* by Saviour Pirotta.

Artwork:
Tom Price age 8, page 7; William Kemp age 5, page 16.

Puppets:
Gingerbread Man by William Kemp age 5; Princess by
Tamika Mclean age 5.

Contents

Different kinds of puppets

Puppets are dolls that can be made to move. They are worked in different ways.

◀ Some puppets are worked by pulling strings.

▶ This puppet is worked by sticks called rods. When you move the rods, the puppet moves.

4 puppets move strings rods

► **Glove** puppets move with your hand.

▼ Some puppets are worked in front of a light. They make a **shadow** on a screen.

Look at the puppets in the pictures. Which one do you like best and why?

glove   shadow

Investigating puppets

Connor's class are looking at puppets.
There are string and glove puppets.

▲ The puppets are made of different materials.
The clown's nose is made of wood.
What other materials can you spot?

materials   wood

Connor draws the clown puppet. He labels it and thinks about how it works.

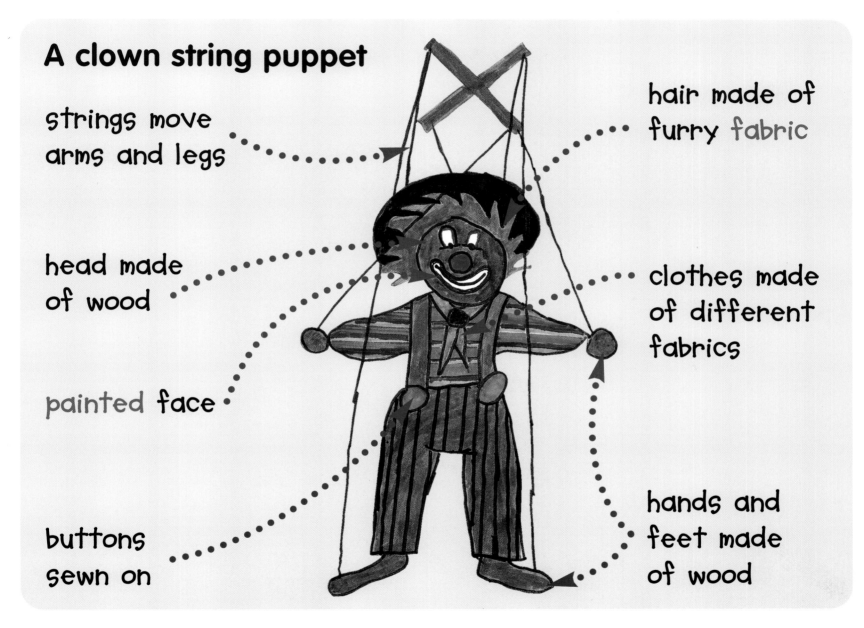

A clown string puppet

strings move arms and legs

hair made of furry fabric

head made of wood

clothes made of different fabrics

painted face

buttons sewn on

hands and feet made of wood

Which of the puppets would you draw?

labels   fabric   painted

Using a template to make a puppet

Eve is making a pencil puppet.

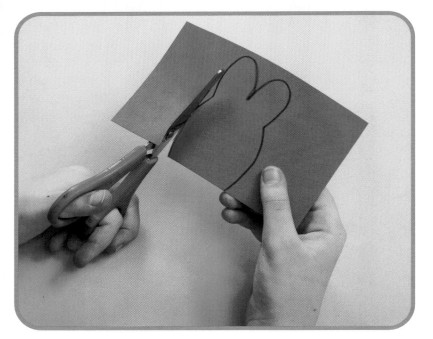

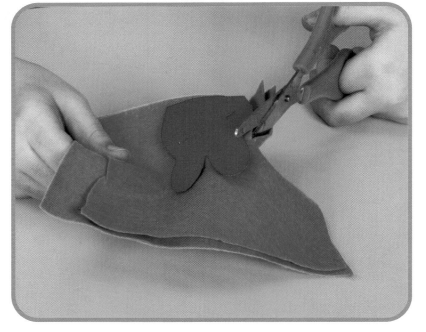

▲ **Eve draws a rabbit's head on card. She cuts the head out to make a template.**

▲ **She pins the template on two pieces of cloth and cuts through both pieces. This gives her two heads.**

draws   template   cuts

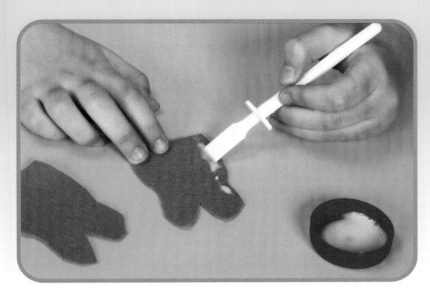

▲ She glues round the edge of one head, leaving the neck free. She presses the other head on top.

Materials and tools
• pen • pencil • card
• scissors • cloth in different colours • glue

▲ Eve makes a face for her puppet and then slides it on top of her pencil.

Can you think of another way of joining the two parts of the head together? Would this work better than gluing?

presses   joining   9

Making different characters

Many puppets are based on fairy tale characters.
They may be male or female, rich or poor, young or old.

◄ Look at the puppet in the picture. Can you tell which character it is? How? What did the puppet-maker do to make it look like this?

fairy tale characters male female

Look at the puppets in the pictures. What kind of characters are they? What is it about their face and costume that tells you this? Which words would you use to describe them?

royal wicked male female

scary friendly old young

wicked scary friendly

Making finger puppets

Ali's class are making finger puppets.

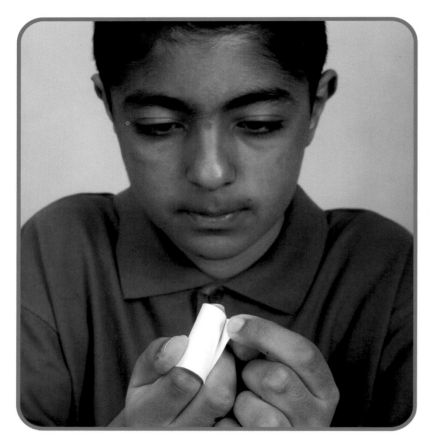

▲ He pins the paper onto the cloth and cuts the cloth to the right size.

▲ Ali rolls a strip of paper round his finger to work out what size the puppet needs to be.

▲ He folds the cloth and staples it.

finger   rolls   strip   size

◀ **He decorates his puppet. What has Ali made? What has Josie made?**

◀ **What did they use to decorate their puppets?**

Materials and tools
- paper • cloth • pins • wool
- sequins • stapler • scissors

What finger puppet would you make?
Who would enjoy using it?

staples   decorates

Puppet shows around the world

Puppet shows are popular in many parts of the world. They are often held on holidays and at other special times of the year. People enjoy watching the puppets.

▲ In China, at New Year, huge dragon puppets dance in the streets.

puppet shows   popular   holidays

▲ Everyone enjoys a Punch and Judy show at the seaside.

▲ In Vietnam, puppet shows take place on the water!

Have you ever been to a puppet show or seen one on television? What did you see? Did you enjoy it? What was good about it?

Planning a puppet show

Ed's class are planning a puppet show for the children in Reception. They will read the story of the Gingerbread Man and act it out with puppets.

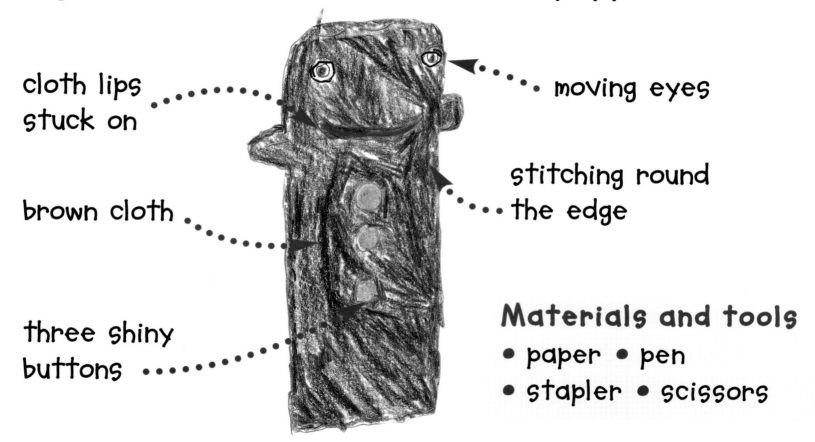

cloth lips stuck on

moving eyes

brown cloth

stitching round the edge

three shiny buttons

Materials and tools
- paper • pen
- stapler • scissors

Ed's Gingerbread Man puppet needs to be strong and fit his hand. He sketches his ideas on a piece of paper.

planning   act   sketches

◄ **Ed makes a mock-up with paper. He draws round his hand to get the right shape and size.**

► **He cuts out the shape through two pieces of paper and staples them together.**

◄ **Ed draws a face and buttons on his mock-up. He has now planned how his puppet will look.**

mock-up   shape

Making a glove puppet

▼ Ed draws round his hand again to make a template for the puppet. He pins it to two pieces of  felt and cuts round it.

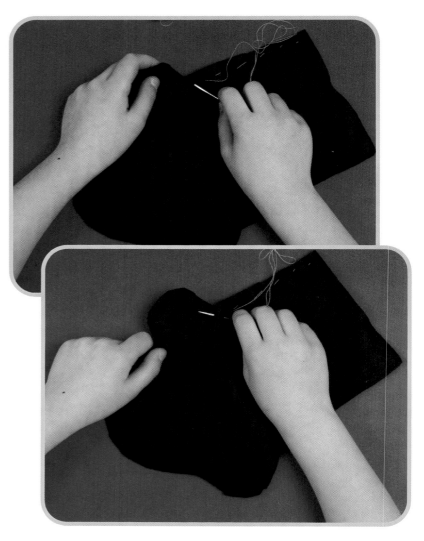

▲ He carefully sews the two pieces of felt together, using a running stitch.

felt sews running stitch improve

Materials and tools
- felt • moving eyes • sequins
- paper • pins • scissors
- needle • thread • glue • pen

WARNING!
Scissors, pins and needles are sharp. Use them with care.

Ed has decorated his puppet. Do you think he is pleased with it? How would you improve it?

"It looks friendly. I think the children will like it."

"The stitches could be stronger. It's coming undone a bit."

19

The puppet show

▶ **The class design a poster on the computer.**

Come to our party!

THE GINGERBREAD MAN
Friday, 22 March
11.30am in the Hall

◀ **Josh reads the story of the gingerbread man.**

design   poster   computer

The puppets bring the story to life. Rose is behind the table working the puppets. The audience cannot see her.

▼ Did the children like the show? How can you tell?

If you put on a puppet show, which story would you tell? What kind of puppets would you make?

audience

Further information for

Possible Activities

PAGES 4-5

Collect puppets and pictures of puppets and make a classroom display. Add to the display by asking children to bring in any puppets they have at home.

Ask children to choose one of the puppets and talk about it to the class, describing the character and how it has been made, how it works and who it is for.

PAGES 6-7

Ask children to choose a puppet from the classroom display, then draw it and label its different parts, showing the range of materials used. Can they suggest other materials which would work just as well?

PAGES 8

Make a pencil puppet like Eve's. Ask children to choose a different kind of head (e.g. a dog or a dinosaur) and to draw it and size it carefully. Does it fit their pencil?

Practise making templates in simple shapes and using them to cut out two thicknesses of cloth. Practise joining the cloth in different ways (e.g. sticking, stapling and stitching). What are the advantages and disadvantages of each?

PAGES 10-11

Brainstorm fairy-tale characters and discuss each one. If it was made into a puppet, how should it look? Ask children to choose a character and make a sketch.

On cards, write some simple descriptions of different puppet 'characters' (e.g. a friendly boy, a silly girl, a hungry wolf). Hand out a card to each of the children and ask them to draw a face that fits the description.

PAGES 12-13

Make finger puppets like Ali and Josie. Make sure there are lots of different materials and fabrics available for the children to use to decorate their puppets (wool, sequins, silk, glitter, etc). Ask the children to assess their own puppets and each other's.

Parents and Teachers

Children could make the different characters from a fairy tale (e.g. Goldilocks and the three bears) and use them to tell the story.

Try making a push-up puppet, using a pencil puppet (see pages 8-9). Make a hole in the bottom of a yogurt pot and push a pencil through it. Add the puppet to the top of the pencil. When you push the pencil up, the puppet appears out of the yogurt pot.

PAGES 14-15

Arrange a visit to a puppet show or invite a local puppeteer to perform in school. Alternatively, show videos of different puppet shows. Discuss the types of puppets and shows. How do they make the stories come to life?

Talk to the children about the importance of puppets in different cultures, making a display of puppets from around the world.

PAGES 16-17

Plan your own puppet show. Who will the show be for and when do you want to perform it? Could it be an end-of-term treat? Write a story for the puppets to act out. It could be based on a fairy tale or nursery rhyme. What kind of puppets would be best and why? Ask children to sketch and mock-up their puppet before making it. Encourage them to think about possible problems, alternatives, etc.

PAGES 18-19

Encourage children to sew their own puppets, and to evaluate the finished puppets. Are they strong enough? Will they do the job the children have made them for?

Further Information

BOOKS FOR CHILDREN

My Puppet Art Class by Nellie Shepherd (Dorling Kindersley, 2003)

Routes to Writing: Recounts: A Day in the Life of a Puppeteer/Our Puppet Week by Claire Llewellyn (Oxford University Press, 2004)

The Crafty Art Book by Jane Bull (Dorling Kindersley, 2004)

The Gingerbread Man by Saviour Pirotta (Hodder Children's Books for WHSmith, 2002)

PAGES 20-21

Write an advertisement for the show. After the performance, ask the children to evaluate their work. Were they happy with the show? Did the audience enjoy it? Would they do anything differently next time?

Index